ENERGIZE YOUR LIFE

ENERGIZE YOUR LIFE

Tap into Your Energy Reserves
and Live in Each Moment

Paul R. Thompson

Author, Nationally Acclaimed Public Speaker, Corporate
Trainer, and Highly Successful Financial Planner

Energize Your Life: Tap into Your Energy Reserves and Live in Each Moment

Copyright © 2014 Paul R. Thompson. All rights reserved. No part of this book may be reproduced or retransmitted in any form or by any means without the written permission of the publisher.

Published by Wheatmark®
1760 East River Road, Suite 145
Tucson, Arizona 85718 USA
www.wheatmark.com

ISBN: 978-1-62787-139-6 (paperback)
ISBN: 978-1-62787-140-2 (ebook)
LCCN: 2014947792

PAUL R. THOMPSON

To purchase additional copies of *Energize Your Life*, to learn more about the author, or to order his first book, *For My Grandchild*, please e-mail the author at paulcfp@aol.com.

I would like to dedicate this book to my wife, my children, and my grandchildren, who enrich my life daily every time I see them, hold them, and think about them. Thank you for your love and support.

A special thanks to my daughter Sharon. Without her urging me forward to publish this, this book would have never made it to a book! She turned ten years of notes into an organized book. It was also her rewriting my notes in my first book, For My Grandchild, *that has gotten me to this moment!*

All proceeds from the sales of this book will go to charities that serve the US Armed Forces.

Contents

· · · · ·

CONTENTS

PART III

Ten Action Steps to Increase Your Positive Energy

PART IV

Summary

Acknowledgments

· · · · ·

I MUST ACKNOWLEDGE THE many hundreds of men and women who have told me how much my work has inspired them and have encouraged me to share with others my insights on the endless amount of energy that I embrace inside myself. Also, I must acknowledge my family: my wife of forty-five years, Karen, who has stood beside me through good times and bad; my sons, Robert and Brian, and my daughters, Adrienne and Sharon, who believe in my abilities and offer a constant source of love and support; my grandchildren, Nicholas, Stephen, Gabrielle, Camryn, Katerina, Christopher, Robert Jr., Broderik, David Jr., and Kolboden, who never fail to keep my energy and zest for life flowing; and finally, all of you out there in this vast world from whom I acquire so much of my energy.

A special thanks to my daughter Sharon. Without her urging me forward to publish this, this book would have never made it to a book! She turned ten years of notes into an organized book. It was also her rewriting my notes in my first book, *For My Grandchild*, that has gotten me to this moment!

Thank you.

ENERGIZE YOUR LIFE

Putting Life in Perspective

Is This You?

· · · · ·

Do you wish that you had more time and energy for the important things in life, like yourself, your family, and friends?

Have you ever found that you are lacking energy or motivation? Do you find that at the end of the day you feel too drained to do anything besides lie on the couch and watch TV?

Are you more likely to be negative about life? Is the glass half-full or half-empty to you?

Are you always wondering what would have happened if only you had chosen a different path in your life?

Do you reach for more than one energy drink or energy bar to help you get through your day?

We often seem to ask ourselves, "Where did the day go?" Eventually, that question turns into, "Where did the weeks and the months go?" As we chase sales quotas and deadlines, raise our families, and strive to be the best we can be, time flits away from us. Our society always seems to be in a rush, and we are the most satisfied if we can get what we want as soon as possible. Despite the way our society runs, there is no quick fix to finding happiness and staying positive. These traits come from a process and the realization that happiness resides inside you.

Too many of us spend a percentage of each day focused on the past or the future. We look back and reminisce about how great we thought life used to be or wonder whether we ought to have taken a different path. When we are not thinking about the past, we are spending a lot of time worrying about the future. Considering our lack of focus on the present, it is not surprising that a large percentage of people feel drained and negative about themselves and their current situations on a daily basis. There are very few people who consistently feel optimistic and energetic every single day of their lives. The average person spends almost no time in the moment, living and loving and enjoying each day as it comes.

This ho-hum lifestyle is unacceptable. We must embrace what's positive. The moment to do that is now!

In the following chapters, you'll be inspired by stories from my own life and from people by whom I have been inspired. You will see how I learned to tap into my energy supply in a way that has helped me and many others. I will pass on my secret of how to be full of energy and optimism all the time.

I believe that as you read about the ways I handle the world around me, you will find out how to tap into your own energy supply.

I am honored that you are letting me be the one to help you find a positive outlook and increase your energy levels. I feel that I can also help you raise your confidence to the next level so that you can enjoy every moment of your life with more energy than you ever knew you had!

This book is not about *changing* you as much as it is about *allowing* you to do something positive for yourself!

My Experiences in Dealing with Adversity

· · · · ·

In times of great stress or adversity, it's always best to keep busy, to plow your anger and your energy into something positive.

—LEE IACOCCA

MANY PEOPLE HAVE faced adversity in their lives. Some let it drag them down by finding relief in drugs, alcohol, or other addictions. Some prefer to keep their heads down and not acknowledge that they have problems, or they let others handle the situation because they cannot or will not do it on their own. I, on the other hand, refused to let my situation keep me down. I envisioned becoming successful, and this inner vision enabled me to grow financially and spiritually through both hard work and positive thinking.

I learned early in life how to deal with some of the

everyday challenges and adversities that life brings. I came from a poor, rural family in South Jersey. With seven children plus my parents, we were always faced with not having enough money. Although my father worked every day of the week for most of his adult life, he barely made enough to put food on the table for all of us. Sometimes, we weren't even fortunate enough for that. My sisters and I would raid nearby farms for fruit or vegetables that hadn't been harvested yet.

At an early age, I was diagnosed with a heart murmur, asthma, and acute allergies, so the doctor told my mother that I couldn't attend gym class at school or compete in sports. Between missing out on these group activities and being at the local free clinic almost every week for shots, I missed a lot of school and was isolated from having strong peer relationships. Back then, there weren't special inhalers to help the asthmatic breathe, and the clinic didn't always have the best doctors. Whenever I had trouble breathing, I was taken to the emergency room; since we were so poor, hospital visits were free.

Often, I would be admitted for at least a day and put in an oxygen tent to pump in cool, fresh air. Within a few hours, I would be back up on my feet and eager to go. The nurses would scold me for racing though the hallways in my wheelchair. As I got older, they tried to give me a sleeping pill after my treatments to get me to rest. I would always slip the pill under my tongue and spit it out as soon as the nurse left the room.

I was always on the brink of failing throughout my school years, not only because I wasn't the greatest student but because I missed so much school. No teacher wanted to fail the "poor Thompson boy," especially since I was so energetic and happy. (I must say that, to this day, my smile is one of my strengths and has gotten me through many hard times!)

Being bullied throughout my school years for being poor made it easy to lose all self-esteem and confidence. The other kids would laugh at me when it was time to pick teams for a sport and say, "Who wants Thompson?"

I'll never forget the school Halloween party when the sympathetic teacher gave me a large paper bag to wear over my clothes along with a cutout face for a mask. Although I pretended I was happy that I had some kind of costume, on the inside, I was crying from the laughter of my peers.

When I was about ten, I decided I was going to earn money, no matter what it took. I took on a paper route and gave my parents most of the money I had earned so that our family could eat, and then I would put some aside for myself. I always had a few quarters in my pockets to buy a lunch at school or snacks for me and my siblings to eat.

Having a paper route was something that I really enjoyed. Not only was I able to make a few dollars from the newspaper company, but I discovered that my positive personality helped me to get more tips. My father had told me when I was very young that I would be successful if I served people. This interaction with people and concept of service with a smile was good not only for my wallet, but also for my self-esteem and, years later, for my business.

Some of my customers who knew of my family's home situation would give me words of encouragement that kept me going when the rest of my world seemed bleak. Even at that point, people were telling me that I was an inspiration and trustworthy.

When I was a teenager, one of my paper-route customers brought me to a junior fraternal organization that did community projects. Having interactions with people who were encouraging and not judging me based on socioeconomics was another boost in my life. As an added bonus, we were helping people who were in the same situation or even worse off than I was.

Around this time, I also worked in a garden apartment complex as a part-time gardener and clean-up guy where I did odd jobs and learned how to use different types of tools. When I was sixteen, I pedaled a portable ice cream cart throughout Ocean Grove, New Jersey, for an entire summer. It was such a great feeling to see children racing toward me at top speed when they heard my bell, and I loved talking to the many varieties of people who inhabited the shore towns in the summer.

At age seventeen, I acquired a more traditional ice cream truck, and, from early morning until the sun set, I would ring the bell. On my days off, usually Sundays, I would help my dad paint houses, which was his occupation. I learned a lot about the workings of business and dealing with people from those moments I spent with my father.

To work on my health problems, I created my own workout program to strengthen my body, especially my lungs. I built my arms up by moving my father's heavy forty-foot wooden ladder around the houses we painted, often using the paint cans as additional weights. I also began a running regimen with my dog, Rusty, and by the time I was eighteen, I was running four miles a day!

Considering that I had spent most of my childhood in and out of the hospital, these physical exertions were incredible successes for me. I no longer needed the clinic, and I didn't have major asthma problems any longer. I found out that my heart murmur was actually quite common and not as much of a problem as I had feared. I had no desire to be sickly. I had a fire inside me that wanted more than an invalid's life, pushing me forward to achieve more, acquire more, and *live*!

My next goal was to become a soldier. By working with my father and running with my dog, I strengthened my body enough that I could successfully join the US Marine Corps. Although those days of boot camp were grueling, I took away some extraordinary memories of my time there.

During my three-year term of service with the marines, I was shipped to Vietnam as part of the first deployment troops to make an amphibious landing. After thirteen months of nightmares and too many bad memories, I finally left Vietnam with sergeants' stripes and an honorable discharge. I married the woman of my dreams, settled down in a tiny house with her, watched our family grow with the births of my four children, and plugged away at life until I could achieve the goals and dreams that I wanted for myself.

I'm telling you this to emphasize that, no matter what adversity you face, there's always hope to overcome most of life's obstacles, particularly if you have a goal and the will to see it through. I had adversity in my life, including being from a poor family and having health problems, and I handled these trials by establishing goals and being determined to achieve these goals, no matter what.

Positive Energy

·····

The energy of the mind is the essence of life.
—ARISTOTLE

FOR YEARS, PEOPLE have asked me, "Where do you get your energy from?"

I am willing to share how to tap into your energy sources, to encourage you to feel more positive about your life and your interactions with people, and to persuade you to reach even higher for your dreams, whether they be about love, success, happiness, or all of the above.

Most people buy books or audio files or attend seminars on motivation, success, and self-improvement because they're looking for a magically easy way to be energized and happy in a negative world. Unfortunately, the moments of positive energy experienced while listening to these sessions doesn't usually go beyond your daily life.

Some people constantly look for a way to improve not only their own actions and performances but also everyone else's around them. Please realize that your own full potential and happiness has to be in place before you can consider making others happier or more productive. Once you have achieved personal inner peace and fulfillment, those qualities overflow, making it natural to spread positive thoughts, actions, and motivation around. You should acknowledge these outward-reaching desires, choose the positive path, and move forward.

Upon embracing the ideas of positive energy, you quickly find the strength, energy, enthusiasm, and positive outlook required to enjoy every aspect of life, family, friends, and career. The key to achieving and maintaining a high energy level begins with the personal belief that you have control of the energy flow that affects all aspects of your life. Every moment is filled with positive and negative energy thoughts. Choosing the positive energy path more often guarantees that your energy levels will be higher rather than expending energy fighting those things that are beyond your control. To choose that positive path, one must learn to rethink each moment in terms of what its energy impact is.

Every day, each person interacts with numerous people who are affected by something as simple as a smile or a warm greeting. Many times, people will smile in response. The cycle of happiness continues as those people interact with additional people, sharing a similar smile. It's a beautiful, constant cycle that can start with you. I hope that my readers will reach out and help someone else.

Since the power of positive thinking has impacts and benefits in my own life, it seemed only natural that those around me wanted to share in this knowledge. The power in these ideas overwhelmed me when I started putting my thoughts down on paper. I would write them down, leave them for a while, and come back to them to feel the positive energy. Then, I was immediately back in the optimistic mind-set I try to focus on consistently. Even natural daily distractions and the need for breaks are overcome by this energy!

One of my favorite movies is *Groundhog Day* starring Bill Murray. He portrays a character destined to relive a day of his life every day until he learns the lesson that will enable him to become a better person. He goes through this day over and over again, and he must redo each of his mundane life choices until he perfects each skill or behavior in a way that improves his character. Initially, he thinks he is being punished by reliving each day but begins to realize that each new day is a gift, a chance to start something positive and new As he molds his personality into being more of who he wants to be, he redeems himself in his own eyes and in the eyes of society and, from this, he finds happiness in his life. The movie clearly demonstrates how human nature remains the same unless we actively try to change ourselves.

At some point in our lives, we all count on the future to solve our problems. This is evident in the way we will daydream unrealistically about how our futures will turn out. Consider this: If we're always waiting for a future event to make us happy, we're not living in the moment. We are not really living until we visualize a dream or goal and actively achieve it.

When I was a corporate trainer in the financial planning industry, I would teach other financial planners how to ask their clients about their goals differently from how they're accustomed to asking them. In my own career, I promoted people financially through different techniques of visualization to achieve their future goals.

I've been on hundreds of interview with financial planners in the field over the last thirty years in a management position, but I've rarely seen them actually get their prospective clients to visualize their goals. It's not enough to just ask a question, take down the answer, and then move on to their recommendations. The average planner spends no more than three to five minutes on a client's goals. For you to be both committed and disciplined to a financial goal, you need to feel that those goals are as important as the endless "wants" that pop up each day that take a toll on our spending money.

In the same way, consider three goals to achieve. One goal today was to find more energy, wasn't it? Movement toward that goal has begun with the opening of this book. To continue along that path, make the moments spent in understanding the message within to be a permanent part of your life. Open this book periodically to whichever section was most enjoyable, and read it again. By doing this, more ideas will come from the extra mental boost received by the rereading. My goal is for my readers to benefit from the lessons, tools, and insights that I've learned and compiled here. Although this book isn't the complete answer to a successful and energetic life, it's a good start. Other motivational tools will continue the boost. There is no need to rely on false energy obtained through chocolate, coffee, and energy drinks.

After all, *you* are the only real solution to achieving and maintaining personal energy levels.

Yourself

...

...ose *who believe in the*

—ELEANOR ROOSEVELT

...hard work and devotion it

...nd every one of my dreams,

...ent resulted from maintain-

...s of my dreams and using

...n and inspiration. I move

...s in order to keep me moti-

...a particular goal.

...rive lags at times, I summon

...tive results of goal achieve-

...I wanted a luxury car, a large

house in an affluent area, and a pool. I also wanted

to be known as an inspirational leader and a suc-

cessful businessman. I kept those images in a special

corner of my mind and dealt with each day's challenges as they presented themselves until I was able to achieve the success I wanted. f you envision what you want in your own life, wrap your dreams and goals in an appealing little compartment in your mind and focus on these positive images when you are down. This compartment also insulates against the negativity that flows through our minds at times. Consider this: Have you heard the following words directed at you?

"Quit daydreaming!"

"You'll never make it."

"You were not born with a silver spoon."

"It's time to face reality!"

These admonitions are just a few of those that bombard us from well-meaning family, friends, and even strangers. In their own life experiences, they have seemingly been programmed to believe the negativity, and they will share their negative viewpoints with anyone who has announced the excitement of having a dream. I would advise that you should stop trying to be what everyone else wants you to be and be who *you* want to be. Realize that people are always going to have an opinion of you, your car, your house, your friends, or any other aspect of your life. While it may be their right to have an opinion, it is not their right to stop you from being who you really are. When feelings of negativity arise, regroup and remember that you come first; no one can take away your positive feelings.

Although there are times when there is no choice but to listen to other people's opinions of you (such as during a supervisor's evaluation), remember that, regardless of whatever critiques they may give you, their opinions doesn't have to drain your positive energy. It's only their opinion, after all. People have told me that they actually changed their plans because someone else gave them their opinion, and they listened to them instead of doing what they had originally planned to do. Know that all of the extra schooling in the world won't mean anything unless you are able to communicate your message in a positive, upbeat format. Getting personal and yet staying professional is often part of the job and is not usually covered in a training manual.

From the moment you wake up, your mental attitude will determine the way your day will unfold. With this in mind, find something positive in the mirror as you perform your daily ablutions. Starting your day with an affirmation toward your body and yourself will not only increase your self-esteem, but also make your day seem more positive. If you wake up in the morning and feel drained, that is a sure sign that you need to rethink and revise the way you view your life.

A friend told me about a breathing exercise she

had learned, in which you inhale deeply through your nose and think, "Yes." Then, you slowly exhale through your mouth, thinking, "Thank you." Such a simple exercise, and yet it works to refocus your mind on the things that matter. Try it, especially when you are feeling particularly stressed or emotionally low.

To give you a quick fix of energy when you're down, I suggest that you call or text a supportive friend who will lift your spirits. True friends are those who will rally around you and when you reach out to get a positive energy boost. In return, you will be there for them, as well, when they are having their own rough moments. Another way to get energy quickly is to reach out to a stranger and do something nice, such as smiling and wishing them a good day. These interactions make you feel better and more positive. It's amazing to see the varying reactions I receive from random strangers at a mere smile or cheerful "hello." The reactions range from amazement that they were noticed at all to a surprisingly happy greeting in return.

A good friend of mine is very active in projects within his church community. When I listen to him talk about these projects, I can feel his energy charging the air around him like a jolt of electricity. For example, every year for Thanksgiving they work in a kitchen as the "certified" stuffers. He loves telling others how hundreds of poor and needy people are given a good meal because serving others is much more fulfilling than to sit at home in front of the TV.

As you work toward remaining positive, you will have many moments when you will get knocked down, worn out, and dumped on by energy-drainers, such as people, circumstances, and what your perception of the world is. Be assured that this is a normal process of life. Remember it's how you respond to adversity and how much you believe in yourself and your ability to bounce back (and bounce back higher!), that determines how easily you can defeat pessimists. Mentally visualize their negative opinions coming in and leaving just as swiftly. Practice this frequently, and you will not only keep your precious energy supply intact, you will also have a lot of fun with the images you can conjure. If you are susceptible to others' opinions, this initial process of not letting their criticisms affect you may take time to become accustomed to. Just as you learn an exercise program, you have to learn the ways of thinking and feeling so that the end result is maintaining a positive outlook on life.

Believe that you can, and you will. Believe you have an endless supply of energy, and you will. Believe that you can overcome the negativity of others, and you will. This doesn't happen by magic; it happens by having the mind-set not only to live fully in each of life's moments, but also to believe in the power of your positive thoughts 100 percent. Simply believe in yourself and your decisions, and you will love the new you who is happy and confident and full of energy! You will be the person you really want to be as long as you believe in yourself.

For those who don't have a specific dream to focus on, start every day by thinking about what makes you feel good and energized and what you are blessed with. Focus on the positive aspects of your life. Of all the things that comprise your life, what do you like to do? I feel fortunate to have worked over the last thirty years with veterans' groups. We go to VA hospitals and sponsor events for the disabled veterans, taking the time to express gratitude for what they sacrificed for our country. I've had the opportunity of spreading joy to their lives while also counting my own blessings—I still have both feet and arms, am not confined to a wheelchair, and am so thankful to be healthy and whole.

Whether I'm working with the veterans or simply being around other people who don't have the health I have, each encounter helps me to appreciate my life. If you are looking to increase your positive energy, I would encourage you to work as a volunteer for a local health organization, like a heart institute or cancer society. My family and I always raised money for the Juvenile Diabetes Research Fund by participating in their yearly walkathons. We did this in honor of my older daughter who has had diabetes since she was nineteen months old.

I can guarantee you that by working with these organizations, you'll raise your awareness level and be more thankful for every moment that you are able to get up and get going. Work on consciously feeding your mind positive energy and images by being involved with these organizations, and you'll be amazed at the results.

Superhuman powers are attributes that comic book creators are expert at giving their characters. While you may not be able to bend steel with your laser vision or leap tall buildings in a single bound, viewing life positively increases your daily amount of energy. It's not just the muscle you build up from strength-training exercises that will keep you supplied with energy. Positive thoughts and emotions will be your strength.

Living for Future Moments

·····

Live for the moment, but also live for future moments.

—KAREN THOMPSON

EVERY TIME I travel, I usually carry with me a small book from Outward Bound called *Book of Readings*. I read it when I need inspiring thoughts to help me stay focused. Every time I read it, I feel myself becoming more motivated to make my dreams happen before it's too late. To have no regrets is a great goal in life, whether that includes making amends with a loved one or buckling yourself into the harness of a parachute.

Once, I was conducting a training session with a group of sales representatives in Washington state. During one of the breaks, I looked over a *Book of Readings* story of an adventure, and I was motivated to try something new. After the seminar, I drove down to Oregon to do some sightseeing, and I decided to climb a few hundred feet to the summit of Mount Hood.It was incredible and invigorating to be at the very top of that mountain and to survey the gorgeous horizon before me. After I descended, I called my wife to tell her of my feat. The quote at the beginning of this chapter is exactly what she said to me. It's not that she doesn't want me to have a good time; she is more concerned that I be careful.

I've been known to fall or injure myself at times. I have never claimed to be athletic or graceful, but I am quite enthusiastic about new, exciting activities. As soon as I recover from each adventure, I'm ready to capture the thrill of life again. I realize that time flies so fast, and each moment is precious. That's why I think that even if you have doubts, you should at least try a new experience. I'm sure it will be one of the best decisions you will make.

Whether you've been defeated by adversity in the past or enhanced and enriched by an experience in the present, it's always exciting to look toward the future and live in the moment. It's not that the past is irrelevant. Generally speaking, life can only be under-stood backward, but in order for you to go forward with your life it must be lived in the moment as often as possible.

Consider the instances in your life where you feel

regret for what happened at that time. Know that you have to learn to live without regrets because by experiencing life's lessons, you are becoming a stronger person. If you're spending too much time dwelling on the past, you're wasting the moments that exist in the present. Some people find wisdom from their failures and successes; this provides them with confidence to make more positive choices about their futures. Stop for a moment and reflect on your life no matter how old you are. What would you do differently with your life if you were given the chance to do it again?

As a grandparent, I find that I am reliving my past as a father. For a large part of my children's early lives, I was working two and sometimes three jobs at a time: as a financial planner, a speaker, and a manager. This ensured that my wife could be home with our four children. Most nights, I would come home just in time to tuck them in, but every Saturday I would spend the day with them while my wife went shopping. Sometimes, though, twenty years later, normal guilt feelings surface, and I say to myself, "If only I had ..." Then I remind myself, "Stop! It's gone!" I had a chance to do better for my family, to make our lives better by working harder, and I chose that path. I realize that I did fully enjoy every precious moment I had with my kids. Now that I am a grandparent, I have more time to do what I want to do with the next generation of Thompsons while my own kids work and give us the opportunity to spend time with their kids. I get to take my grandchildren to the park, on camping trips, and to various other activities that I didn't get the chance to do with my children. Plus, I don't have the stress of being a disciplinarian.

In the January/February 2000 issue of *Modern Maturity* magazine, they include an article called "Twenty-Five Ways to Reinvent Yourself." Three of their suggestions are closely in line with this book's message. The first is to create a mission statement of your life in twenty-five words or fewer. List your hopes and dreams of what you want your life to accomplish. It's an incredibly motivating statement to write, and it will keep you focused on your future.

The second is to write your eulogy by answering the question, "What would you want people to say about you after you're gone?" Will you be remembered as quiet and sweet, or as adventurous and happy? Or will you be remembered as miserable and angry, or as negative and sad?

The third way to reinvent your mind-set is to live in the present, not the past. This is often one of the hardest for most people to find the courage to change. Sometimes people live in the past as if they can hold on to it by not letting go. Consider this, though: you can't hold on to something that's not there anymore. That is why it's called the past. Some people feel that to let go of the past is to be alone and vulnerable, and they let their fears control their destinies and their faults weigh them down. Some of us spend a great deal of time remembering what *used* to be instead of looking toward what *could* be.

Positive memories are the ones in which to revel. Hold onto the moments that lift your spirits. However, your entire day should not be wrapped up in memories, so minimize the amount of time that you spend in your memory. Squeeze in only enough memory-moments to feel the positive, energizing feelings you associate with them.

Through the years, I've come across people who looked tired, bored, or wanted to be anywhere else than where they were. Upon approaching them and striking up a conversation, I found that they lacked any desire to be in the moment. Once I would ask them where they would rather be or what they would prefer to be doing, I could sense their minds perking up. Specific questions that got their senses aroused mentally got them lit up and speaking enthusiastically about these new and positive thoughts.

Years ago, I was having a very low day, and I couldn't find my extra reserve of energy. (We all have days when our energy levels are low—it's normal.) My younger daughter noticed that I wasn't myself and, wanting to help, wrote a poem for me titled "P.T." When I read it, my spirits and energy levels lifted back to what is normal for me, even as it put a tear in my eye. To this day, I keep her poem with me and take it out periodically to revel in the positive message within. I have included this poem at the end of this book to give you a chance to experience some of the positive feelings it contains. I would also mention that my daughter is the one who has pushed me to get this book out of the file cabinet to share the message of having an energized and happy life.

Ask someone to give you a few short sentences or comments about how you have affected them in some positive way in the course of your relationship. If nothing else, create one for yourself about positive things you have done; you will still be surprised at how many lives you've touched.

Think about it. Anyone who has ever done volunteer work or a simple good deed has definitely felt the energy boost that comes from knowing that they have helped someone. Talking to someone, listening, and understanding are ways that you are helping. When you help someone, your energy level soars along with theirs.

Whether you've been defeated by adversity in the past, or enhanced and enriched by an experience in the present, it's always exciting to look toward the future and live constantly in the moment. It's not that the past is irrelevant. Generally speaking, life can only be understood backward, but in order for you to go forward with your life and enjoy the moment, it must be lived "in the moment" as often as possible. By reminding people that they are, in fact, living in the present, you are helping them to remember that we all have goals and dreams, and that every moment we live is precious. These are the moments I'm talking about.

Positive
by Norman Vincent Peale

If you want to get somewhere, you have to know
where you want to go and how to get there.
Then never, never, never give up.

The secret of life isn't what happens to you,
but what you do with what happens to you.

Help other people to cope with their problems,
and your own will be easier to cope with.

Never use the word impossible again.
Toss it into the verbal waste bucket.

Self-trust is the first secret of success.
So believe in and trust yourself.

Stand up to your obstacles and do something about them.
You will find that they haven't half the strength you think they have.

Joy increases as you give it
and diminishes as you try to keep it for
yourself.
In giving it, you will accumulate a deposit of
joy
greater than you ever believed possible.

How you think about a problem is more
important
than the problem itself—so always think
positively.

Go at life with abandon; give it all you've got.
And life will give all it has to you.

Part II

Overcoming Emotional Obstacles

Energy Drainers

· · · · ·

While we may not be able to control all that happens to us, we can control what happens inside us.

—BENJAMIN FRANKLIN

ENERGY DRAINERS ARE like holes in your body that need to be plugged up and stopped. They originate in your mind and filter down through your body, affecting your thoughts and actions, and, especially, your interactions with people around you. There are many words, phrases, and emotions that drain your energy sources. An energy-draining phrase is often used to describe why someone isn't feeling positive or optimistic and is the scapegoat for the negativity inside people. Consider these:

"As soon as my ship comes in…"
"I'm going to win the lottery…"
"When my children grow up…"
"I'll do what I want to do when I retire…"

Sound familiar? Sure they do. There are numerous words and phrases that are used often and tend to be energy drainers. Here are some words and phrases you find creeping into your dialogue daily. I have found these to be major energy-drainers:

- But…
- Should…
- If…
- Can't…
- I'll try…
- You're wrong…
- You'll never make it…
- I'm too tired…
- Why me?
- It's impossible for me to do this.

Try to eliminate these words and thoughts from your mind. In fact, address these energy drainers as soon as they appear so that they are unable to leak into your subconscious and affect your day. When negative thoughts enter our minds, they become parasitic in nature, attaching themselves to every thought and emotion we have. They may start out small, but as we focus on them, they become larger. Eventually, they make us weak and depressed and unwilling to turn our thoughts in a more positive direction. Perhaps you can't get rid of them completely, but you can definitely stop dwelling on them and giving them your energy.

The ability to make logical, rational decisions is impeded greatly by negative thoughts, and I often tell people not to make decisions when they are in a depressed, angry, or feeling-lousy kind of mood. By stepping away from the stressor, whatever it may be, they are able to stabilize their emotions and think more rationally so that they can address the situation later, with a different frame of mind. Eventually, when they have had time to rise above the negative thoughts and emotions, they find that the decision they made during the period of distraught feelings is drastically different from what they would now do with a more positive mind-set.

For example, when the stock market fell several years ago, I found it hard to stay positive when I couldn't tell my clients what was going to happen to their investments in the near future. Rather than panic or become morose, I spoke to each and every worried client and friend who called me and conveyed a feeling of positivity to them, assuring them that everything would be okay once the market settled. Sure enough, within a few weeks, the market bounced back, and everyone breathed a huge sigh of relief. If I had reacted to the drop negatively, spreading doom and gloom and worrying unnecessarily about something out of my control, my clients may have been reluctant to trust me with their plans and dreams once the market stabilized.

You will notice that the more positive interactions you have with people, the better you will generally feel about your own life. Begin to interact more with your neighbors and your community, whether it's through a club or organization or simply by getting outside more and meeting people in the neighborhood. Get involved with people and stay positive. Interact with people with genuine interest and they will respond in favor. You will find people out there who can share their supplies of positivity and may also turn out to be good friends.

When my family was growing up in rural New Jersey, all nine of us lived in a small, one-hundred-year-old house, hardly more than what the average person now would call a run-down shack. We shared three bedrooms, and at night, you could hear the scuttling rats that inhabited the dark recesses of our home. Fortunately, a good friend at that time told me that I could achieve owning a mansion if I really wanted to. For years, I thought he was referring merely to having a larger home, so I worked harder than ever and strived for that elusive "mansion on the hill" where my family and I would reside happily. It wasn't until years later that I realized what he really meant: that my mansion is whatever and wherever I have achieved my goals and dreams such that my family and I are safe and happy.

Eventually, once my children were grown, I built a large house in an upscale community. We sold the home my family had lived in for over twenty years and moved into a brand-new one. Were we happier in our new home? In some ways, yes, we were happier because I had achieved a major goal of mine. Yet, it didn't matter how large the house was, or how big my backyard was. It was my happy place, where I could be with those I love and enjoy family gatherings and other social events.

When you visualize what you want to happen to you in the future, it becomes more attainable. Simply by envisioning your future goals, whether it's to become rich, to buy a house, or simply to have a nest egg for your retirement,you will feel more positive and capable of achieving them.

Perspective on
Everyday Occurrences
·····

*It might be raining outside, but in your heart
you can have sunshine.*

—PAUL THOMPSON

I HAVE READ COUNTLESS books and articles about
how to improve my energy levels and reduce the
amount of stress in my life. I internalize these ideas,
filing them away until I need them. In order to fully
achieve a better way of living your life, you need to
have the determination to achieve your goals.

From the time we're babies, we're exposed to the
ideas of right and wrong determined by how those
caring for us perceive these standards. As we get older,
we obtain more information about right and wrong
from books, television, and people we encounter in

school, work, and social interactions. We discover that what is right for some people isn't necessarily what works for other people. The common expression "Would you rather be right or be happy?" may help to stop you from draining your energy reserves fruitlessly. Think about the endless amounts of energy that have been wasted on trying to be right. Too many times we expend too much of our energy trying to find supporting evidence for our "right," when a simple concession would be so much healthier for us.

In order to experience more of what life has to offer, it's important for you to give everyone and everything a chance. Many relationships that we develop make us stronger; we need to make room for positive people and events in our lives. Different people and experiences lead you to positive experiences and thoughts, whether for a reason or a season or even a lifetime.

Think before you speak. I believe if more people thought about what they were going to say before they said it, there would be an incredible drop in the number of conflicts in the world. When you feel overwhelmed by a negative person or situation, practice some breathing exercises to maintain your positive energy. Take several deep breaths and relax your body any time you must respond to someone who has offended you. Visualize waving goodbye to the negativity that tries to fester in your brain. Once you become accustomed to doing so, you'll find yourself automatically reaching for more positive feelings and thoughts. Sticking with a new plan or behavior will eventually become effortless if you commit to using it every day.

It seems that whatever habits we picked up as children from the people around us stay with us for a long time. We tend to follow our parents' beliefs and negativity or their hope and positive mind-sets. The environment that we are raised in often determines our general outlook on life, whether it's an atmosphere of failure, negativity, hope, or optimism. Changing our thought patterns as we grow gives us new opportunities to see life differently from before. Change helps us to think new thoughts and develop new interests in life, which, in turn, help us to increase the amount of positivity in our lives.

In my industry I'm told that most people prefer financial planners who show genuine care about their welfare and success over planners who demonstrate only a higher rate of return. I'm proud of the fact that I have had relationships with my clients for years, some for almost three decades. To me, that is success.

Some people wake up on a rainy day and think to themselves, "What a miserable day!" They get dressed, eat breakfast, go to work, and tell everyone they see that it's a miserable day. Their shoulders hunch, they avert their gazes, and they speak in monotone voices.

Eventually, the miserable feelings spread beyond just themselves to whoever is vulnerable enough to listen. Notice that they feel the misery simply because they *perceive it* to be so, not because it is really there.

Don't let that kind of thinking affect you. No, it's not miserable—it's just raining. God is giving energy and life to all things that grow, including you! So what if it's raining? Don't we need rain to keep the beautiful flowers nourished and our reservoirs full? Be thankful for it! Every so often, we may be faced with a summer drought, and then we *pray* for rain. Think about how soft and relaxing the rain sounds on the roof or outside your window as you are lying in bed at night. Sometimes I play rain sounds on my radio in order to relax my body so that I can fall asleep more easily.

The point is that some people always look to blame something outside themselves for their failures or bad moods. It so happens that the weather is the easiest excuse to use. Those who are miserable during the rain are also unhappy when it snows. They will grumble all winter and say they can't wait for summer, and when summer gets here, they complain about how hot it is. When I visit the beach in the summer, some people "relaxing" in the sun are complaining that it's too hot.

Have you considered that using the weather as the key determiner of your day allows an aspect of life you have no control over take control of you? I have overheard people state that they are going to have a horrible week because the weather forecast calls for snow and rain all week. While the weather or the news of the day can initiate the average person's daily conversations, make sure to avoid letting any of their weather-induced negativity influence the positive moments of your day. There are too many other important things to concentrate on (such as your loved ones and friends, your job, yourself, and your role as an important member of society) to be brought down by a weather report. I'm not saying you can ignore a tornado or a blizzard coming, but those events are ones you can deal with and prepare for. Remember to keep your perspective on everyday events, such as the weather, your commute to work, or a conversation with a coworker. These occurrences do not have to determine your mood. Search for the best in the present moment and try not to dwell in worry, fear, anger, or depression. Your mind is pro-grammed to believe what you tell it, whether it's raining or sunny outside.

The spreading of doom and gloom seems worse than the common cold, especially when you're at work. Bad news spreads to the point that people become too paralyzed to do their work. It's all about perspective, how you take events in your life in stride. Helping others, and sharing good feelings with them will not only make you feel much more energized by living in the moment, but your energy will be contagious—even to the person depressed by the weather. You don't have to get yourself into a meditation mind frame to feel positive.

Things Work Out
by Edgar Guest

Because it rains when we wish it wouldn't,
Because men do what they often shouldn't,
Because crops fail, and plans go wrong—
Some of us grumble all day long.
But somehow, in spite of the care and doubt,
It seems at last that things work out.
Because we lose where we hoped to gain,
Because we suffer a little pain,
Because we must work when we'd like to
    play—
Some of us whimper along life's way.
But somehow, as day always follows the night,
Most of our troubles work out all right.
Because we cannot forever smile,
Because we must trudge in the dust awhile,
Because we think that the way is long—
Some of us whimper that life's all wrong.
But somehow we live and our sky grows
    bright,
And everything seems to work out all right.
So bend to your trouble and meet your care,
For the clouds must break, and the sky grow
    fair.
Let the rain come down, as it must and will,
  But keep on working and hoping still.

For in spite of the grumblers who stand
   about,
Somehow, it seems, all things work out.

Compartmentalizing Your Negative Emotions

. . . . .

If you are patient in one moment of anger, you will escape a hundred days of sorrow.

—CHINESE PROVERB

SPENDING YOUR TIME battling negative thoughts drains your energy, as does trying to address every feeling you have. Sometimes, we have more than one negative emotion pulling at us, such as anger and fear, or jealousy and greed. Instead of trying to eliminate all of your emotions, try to focus on one at a time and deal with it.

One of the most important ways for you to maintain your positive feeling is to find positive people and make it a routine part of your day to spend time with them. Those with whom you associate determine not only your stress level but also the levels of positive thinking you have in your brain. Being around negative, stressed people, who dislike objects and people intensely and can't visualize any positive thoughts, is a detriment for you.

When I need to remove myself mentally from a negative person, I visualize myself in the future having success, and my energy level surges upward. Rather than letting the person's words bring my mood down, I picture an invisible shield around me deflecting their words and emotions so that I can maintain my positive outlook. Sometimes, the negativity flows out of a situation. I use the same method to combat it. This enables me to deal more positively with it, whether it's a delayed flight at the airport, traffic on the parkway, a difficult client or colleague or family member, or five tasks needing to be done simultaneously in the office.

When I turned fifty, I felt that I wasn't really enjoying life to the fullest despite maintaining my energy level while I worked two jobs. Although I was making good money working for a large brokerage house as their senior vice president and doing some financial planning, I felt that I would be more fulfilled working only as a financial planner, helping people to reach their goals financially. So, I made a major decision. I resigned as vice president of the brokerage firm and committed to making myself just as successful by working only one full-time job. I opened up an office, hired people to work with me (all family, of course!), and marched forward. The results of that decision have affected my life greatly. My income increased to five times what I was making working two jobs, and my quality of life has moved from merely good to fantastic! Additionally, I gain extra benefits. As owner of my own financial planning firm, I can take time off whenever I want to and put what's important in my life first. Some days, I can take the time to spoil my grandchildren or play a round of golf with my son. I hadn't lost my positive energy, but this change has actually made me feel like I have regained the energy levels I possessed over twenty years ago.

Anxiety, stress, and anger can disrupt our normal objectivity in making a good decision. When we feel stress in our lives, our brain and body are flooded with stress hormones which hamper the function of our brain's logic center. Perhaps you have many negative feelings toward your own job. Maybe you feel that you are more qualified for the job you have, or conversely, that your job is too difficult for what you trained for. Regardless, the way you approach your career determines how successful you are. Even if you cannot presently leave your job, can you find ways to be happy there? Can you reduce the number of negative feelings that you have toward it now?

I ask people what they would like to do for an occupation if they could do anything they wanted with their lives. Generally, their first responses are something like, "I can't even think about what I really *want* to do because I need this job to support me."

"All right," I reply. "But, if money wasn't a factor, what would you really like to do?"

As they consider this and talk through what they would really like to do, I can both see and feel their energy levels increasing through their body language and speech patterns. Spending your working days, your weeks, your entire careers frustrated, angry, or depressed is really giving up a vitally important aspect of your life that you are able to control.

In the financial planning process, we initially sit down with prospective clients and try to assess their goals and solve their financial problems. Before a prospect becomes a client, I have to give them reasons to trust my financial guidance. Without this key aspect of trust, our work would be hampered. One of the ways I build this trust is to share some of my energy by showing them that I care for them and their needs. Recently, a client told me, "I could feel that I could trust you because of the high level of energy you generate, and I can feel that you care." It's a personal goal of mine to finish phone conversations by leaving people smiling. People become energized and positive almost immediately when they not only think about changing but actually do something to precipitate that change.

Do you need a boost in your attitude toward your work? Visualize what you would like to be doing. Can you see yourself reaching that goal? What would it take to make your dream job become your real job? Can you do something today?

Not too many in this world are born rich. In fact, only a small percentage of people go from birth to death as "rich." We make our own riches, whether they be material or spiritual, and it is up to you to decide how "rich" you want your life to be. Remember that money isn't everything; relationships, positive thinking, and hard work are.

As I mentioned, I grew up incredibly poor in rural New Jersey, and my mother and father worked hard to clothe and feed a family of nine. There were days when we literally had nothing, and yet we were happy. How? We had each other, and we had many fun things to do and explore. We made up games, used our imaginations, and chased each other through the neighborhood. Perhaps times were a bit different when I was growing up, but the point is that you can be happy no matter what amount of money you earn. Just talk to someone who is unemployed, and you will realize how valuable your happiness actually is. Count your blessings.

Stress is an unwelcome appendage. For most of

us, it is a daily part of our lives. Forms of stress come in all shapes and sizes, from what you want to eat for lunch or what you should plan to be feeding a small dinner party. You may stress over relationships or even minor decisions, such as wearing the red tie or the paisley one. Most of us experience most of our stress from our jobs. Stress causes your thoughts to become disjointed, making you become anxious because you are unable to think clearly. Not only is your mind affected, but your body experiences the negative effects of stress as well. You may suffer from sleep deprivation, lack or gain of appetite, and various other bodily malfunctions. Figure out how to manage the stress in your life so that you can move forward more freely.

Do Less
Author Unknown

Do less thinking
And pay more attention to your heart.
Do less acquiring
And pay more attention to what you already
have.
Do less complaining
And pay more attention to giving.
Do less controlling
And pay more attention to letting go.
Do less criticizing
And pay more attention to complimenting.
Do less arguing
And pay more attention to forgiveness.
Do less running around
And pay more attention to stillness.
Do less talking
And pay more attention to silence.

Make Your Time
More Enjoyable
· · · · ·

At a moment's notice, you can summon all the energy you'll ever need to enjoy your life's moments.

—PAUL THOMPSON

SOMEONE ONCE TOLD me that it is probably easier for me, personally, to take a moment to stop and breathe since I am so accustomed to finding positive energy in everyday moments. This isn't completely true. Yes, I may be more aware of living in the moment than others since I do concentrate on using it in my own life, but I'm no different from anyone else in how my mind works. I get bombarded with negative thoughts at times, and then I do what I recommend to others to do: I seek out authors and

CD's,and people who are not only as energized as I am but also even more so. I also have a core list of friends that I can call to bring my energy level up no matter what hour of the day or how long it's been since we last spoke. I recommend these practices because they work very well for me.

Most people review their day before they get out of bed in the morning, making a mental list of what they have to do and who they need to see.

"I have to see..."

"I have to do this..."

The lists can become overwhelming on some days, but by dwelling on your task list or how stressful your appointments may be, you're liable to make *any* situation that arises more stressful than it could be. Dwelling on what's to come will also make it harder to rise from the comfortable warmth of your blanket and bed. An exercise that I can guarantee will work is to simply lie in bed, run through some of the events or interactions scheduled for that day, take a deep breath through your nose, and think, "Yes." Then, slowly exhale as you picture the words, "Thank you." This puts perspective on your life and encourages the idea that sometimes these stressors make each day unpredictable and fun. I always look for the amusement and spontaneity in stressful moments because I continue enjoying my day.

There are twenty-four hours in a day and seven

days in a week. Try to readjust your schedule to make room for what's important in your life. Instead of trying to do everything all at once, spread your obligations and duties around. Not only will it give you the feeling of having more time, but you also won't feel the unrelenting pressure of that persistent rat race.

Emotions form a crucial part of our mind-sets. Obtaining control of your emotions puts you that much closer to living each moment fully. Not only will your outlook on life improve, but your energy levels will increase. Take each day and obstacle as it comes and turn negative words and thoughts into positive words and ideas. A recent college graduate may become frustrated that he or she has not acquired a position in a company two months after graduation, or a businessman may feel defeated that he didn't net the big sale that would have solidified his position as CEO. In situations such as these, rather than feeling failure, tell yourself that you've only suffered a minor setback.

It can be hard to avoid negativity in your everyday life, whether it's coming from your own feelings or from other people. Sometimes, it seems like no matter what you know about positive thinking, no matter how many mental exercises you do to reinforce your positive energy, or no matter how many times a day you tell yourself to pause and reflect on the moment, the negative thoughts lie in wait to barrel through your energy reserves.

Stop!

Take a moment. Live a moment. Breathe.

Whenever I am able to go to one of the two Veterans' Hospitals in Maryland, I enjoy the experience incredibly. While I am there to bring some comfort with a few gifts and empathize with the veterans, I find that I benefit more than the veterans because of *their* positive energies. Despite their situations, they have a contagious positive energy. For example, one day, most of the men we visited had lost one or more limbs, a terrible loss. Yet, these vets were the most optimistic guys—not just in the facility but also in my acquaintance! Instead of poor attitudes about what they had lost, I heard them say, "As soon as they release me and I can walk on my stilts, I'm going back to school," or "I can't wait to be released so I can start a new career," or "My family is behind me, and that's the best thing in the world!"

When you feel as if your day has become overwhelming and the outlook for positive energy seems bleak, I recommend that you give yourself time to pinpoint those negative feelings that are dragging you down. Get out of your office or house and just sit somewhere calming for fifteen to thirty minutes a day (or even just five minutes is a good starting point!). During this time, try to think clear, calming thoughts and use your senses to explore the world around you. Observe how blue the sky is or how fluffy the clouds are. Marvel over the softness of the grass under your feet or how incredible it is that birds can fly so skillfully through the air. Not only will you see the wonders of nature and the surrounding world in a new light, but that time of quiet reflection will enable you to collect your thoughts and feel the comforting rays of positivity shine through once more.

Try not to let a bad moment ruin an entire day, and try to incorporate laughter into your day. No matter what happens today, don't carry it into your tomorrow. The belief that you can live each moment positively, with positive results, is what will enable you to succeed in your life. If you have faith, you won't have fear. Believe in yourself, and the rest will follow.

PART III

Ten Action Steps to Increase Your Positive Energy

Step 1: Leave Your Comfort Zone Behind

. . . . .

Yesterday is a canceled check; tomorrow is a promissory note. Today is ready cash . . . use it!

—Anonymous

A s I mentioned earlier, the fact that you've taken the time to read this book is actually your first step to achieving more energy and happiness in your life. You know that you want answers on how to deal with daily stressors, and you are motivated to find out how to find more energy to carry you through each and every day.

One of the most important components of living a more positive life is to try new things. By leaving the boundaries of your comfort zone, you will find that you have more positive energy than you ever had before, simply because you are pursuing a new avenue which stimulates the mind. Challenge yourself to try something new, especially if it's something that you normally wouldn't do. Much of what we take on in life, whether in relationships or adventurous situations, can leave us either stronger or weaker depending on how we view life.

Imagine a bicycle tire that is slowly leaking air until it finally becomes flat. This is what happens to us when we continue to do the same things every day without looking for new experiences that will enable us to grow and discover ourselves. Join a hiking club, try that appetizer you have always been curious about, or change your hairstyle. Start with something small and work your way up!

Another key to gaining more positive energy is to learn more about yourself. Maybe everyday lifestyles aren't enough to challenge you or to bring you happiness. Think about the things you want out of life, and then distance yourself from negativity and anything that causes you anxiety, stress, or depression.

A positive person feels positive about the world around them. In dealing with a truly positive person, you will feel as if someone opened the window in an otherwise airless room and a fresh breeze has filled the space, one that freshens your mind to be ready to listen and learn and feel. You may feel elated and feel that you can accomplish anything. Their enthusiasm is contagious and changes the entire atmosphere of their surroundings.

What makes these people so positive? Where do they get their energy?

These positive people are those lucky individuals who are truly happy with the lot they've drawn in life. They have made their past, present, and future their own and are committed to sharing the energy they have with those around them. They are the ones who frequently leave their comfort zones and reach out to everything life has to offer with enthusiasm.

While it's good to try to be a positive influence on someone, remember that only someone who wants you to help them can be helped. Many well-intentioned people feel that they have to change a loved one, a friend, their bosses, or their coworkers, for example. Whenever you're concentrating on someone else's faults, problems, or personas, you are not only trying to accomplish an impossible task but you are also draining your emotional energy reserves.

You can't live your moment if you are always worrying about someone else's moments. Work on what you can do for yourself first, and stay out of other people's moments or problems unless they ask for your help. Sometimes people can ask for too much of your energy, especially once they find out that you're more than happy to spend your energy trying to solve their problems.

When I started out as a salesman for Metropolitan Life in 1969, there was a general belief around the office that life insurance couldn't be sold in December. Sure, our manager still had his weekly sales meeting, but you could tell that even he believed that sales would be down at that time. Anyone who also believed in this December theory tended to believe that you couldn't sell life insurance in the summer, either, since everyone was on vacation.

Fortunately, I listened to and believed some of the more successful agents in the office, those who hadn't given over to the negative mind-set of the people around them. The successful agents were those always on top of their business, whose clients bought policies from them any time of the year because they had a need that the agent could address. These agents had an enthusiasm that made them successful, despite the doom-and-gloom of the December theorists.

Enthusiasm is the key to success. Show that enthusiasm to the face in the mirror every morning, show it to random strangers on the way to work or school, and most definitely show it to your family and friends. Remember that enthusiasm is like creamy peanut butter—it spreads. When you see someone who is in a good mood and greets you with a smile and genuine greeting, share your own "peanut butter" and pay that person a compliment immediately. They will tell you that you've made their day. It's a win-win situation.

Starting Today
Anonymous

Starting today:
I'm going to live my life to the fullest.
I'm going to have no regrets for yesterday.
I'm going to forget about all the bad
experience I've in the past.

I'm going to do myself a favor—
To forget about the burdens,
To forget about the pains,
To forget about the hurts.

Starting today:
I won't let anyone tell me that I can't.
I won't let anyone get in my way.
I will do things on my own.
I'm going to be my own best coach,
And I'm going to be a good leader for myself.

Starting today:
I won't waste time on the things that I cannot
change.
I won't waste time trying to change
What's in the past.

I won't waste time trying to be someone
I'm not.
I won't waste time trying to hide my
situation.
I won't waste time worrying about what
people say about me—
Or my situation.

Starting today:
I'm going to live like I won't live again;
I'm going to smile like I won't smile again.
I'm going to do well in everything that I do,
with no regrets.
And I'm going to shape my life for the better.

Step 2: Regain Your Inner Balance

· · · · ·

There are only two days in the year that nothing can be done. One is called yesterday, and the other is called tomorrow. So today is the right *day to love, believe, do, and mostly live.*

—DALAI LAMA

OW DO YOU maintain the inner balance between your dreams and reality? This is one of the biggest challenges you face every day. Without dreams, we may lose all hope and inspiration to go on. Dreams give us that sense of anticipation that we hold on to, even in the face of adversity. Finding the meaning in our lives through our dreams is a core essential to find our inner balance.

When I say "meaning," I'm referring to finding

meaning in our lives and in our everyday interactions with others, we are destined to discover what is really important to us. Use this knowledge to further enrich your life with meaning, and you will notice an incredible difference in your dealings with situations and people.

You are in control of your thoughts and emotions. It's your choice to read this book; it's your choice to follow my suggestions; and it's your choice to live in the moment with a positive attitude and a happier view of life. Our mind-set controls how we react throughout the day. Think about the last time that someone made you angry. How many times did you replay the scenario in your mind, wishing you had said or done something differently to get back at the other person?

When you're confronted with your next negative situation, think or say something about it three times. Stop at three! At first, it's going to be difficult to stop talking about it after three times, but, with practice, it gets easier. By airing out your frustrations and feelings of negativity, you can move forward smoothly with your day because those negative feelings and thoughts are cast out of your subconscious. If you notice other people around you who are venting continuously about something negative that happened, share the three-times rule, and see if it works for them also. You'll be surprised at how easy it is to get rid of not only their negative feelings, but yours as well.

My personal dreams when I was young were basic: speak like an expert; marry a woman who loved me; have a few children; become financially independent; have an expensive house and car; travel; own a successful business; and be loved and respected by friends and family alike. My journey to success wasn't easy, though. It was often filled with doubts, fears, failures, and a lack of confidence. However, I often compare my life to the stock market (which seems appropriate since it's been part of my profession for over thirty years!). If you look at any section of a stock chart, you will see that it's filled with ups and downs. Life is the same way. Throughout the failures and an overall fear of not succeeding, I also experienced many highs, achieved smaller goals, and lived my life honestly and happily. Every time I reached a low point, I would reach deep inside myself and reexamine my goals and dreams so that I could focus on how to get back to positive feelings and regain balance in my life.

At this point in my life, I can honestly say that I have achieved all of my goals. If you honestly believe in yourself and if you have a strong desire to achieve your dreams and goals, then you will. Just as you can easily visualize failure, you can just as easily visualize success. Get and retain a picture in your mind of what your vision of success is. Let it be a beacon to you through the tough times that may come before success occurs.

In some form or another, we all possess a conscience to help us make decisions that will influence our lives in one way or another. You've seen those cartoons showing a cute little devil and an angel pop up on each side of the character. The devilish-looking character is urging the person to do the wrong thing which will lead to negativity, and naturally the good cherub is urging the character to do the right thing, which leads to positivity. Isn't this what we do all the time, although without the imaginary figures on our shoulders? For every decision we make, we go through an internal debate process. When you go to a positive seminar, read an uplifting book, or meet someone who gets you pumped up, you go through the rest of the day thinking in a more positively.

Remember that you are in control of the moments in your life. Make the decision today to be more committed to achieving your goals, achieving higher levels of energy, and maintaining a level of peace. Last, but not least, memorize the "Thank God for Today" creed I've included here so that you can start each day with a feeling that makes you look forward to rising out of bed. You don't have to be in a meditation mind frame to enjoy your moments and hopes and dreams. You just have to look, feel, taste, and desire to capture each moment to the fullest.

Thank God for Today
by Anonymous

This is the beginning of a new day. I can
waste it or use it for good.
What I do today is important because I am
exchanging a day of my life for it.
When tomorrow comes this day will be gone
forever—leaving in its place something I have
traded for it.
I want it to be gain, not loss; good, not evil;
success, not failure; in order that I shall not
regret the price I paid for today.

Step 3: Commit to Being More Positive

·····

You will draw to yourself that which makes you most persistently think about.

—Anonymous

NEGATIVITY IS A part of our world. A long time ago, I decided that when I hear or see negativity, I will let it go right on by and, instead, look for the positive in whatever situation I am in. During conversations with certain colleagues or coworkers whom I know tend to be negative, I will exit the conversation as soon as I feel that any of my positivity will not be appreciated. It saves me from dropping into their negative mind-set and allows me to find a more positive conversation or group of people.

When we encounter other people in our daily

lives, most of us go through the habitual greeting of "Hi, how are you?" Most times, we get a response or a similar greeting in return or, at least, an acknowledgment of their state of mind. Sometimes, though, we get trapped into listening to someone's problems. When they're finished unloading all of their negative baggage onto us, they may say, "Thanks for listening. I feel better already!" They walk away and you are left wondering why you feel horrible all of a sudden. At that point, we may be thinking that a nonresponse is not always a bad thing!

These situations can be a tremendous drain on your energy, especially your emotional energy. You need to bring yourself into your own moment and find out what's happening in your world—and only your world. Don't worry about someone else's problems if those problems are only going to interfere with your happiness, especially when you can't control those circumstances. Listen to what they say, and promptly let it go.

Remember, the more you extend your positive energy to people, the more you will get back in return. Simply listening to another person, reaching out a hand to help them up when they are down, or sharing your resources with them will keep your own emotional energy high. Keep your positive feelings close to you, and continue to enjoy whatever activity you are engaged in.

It is so easy to be caught up in the negativity of people around us because, often, we deeply care for the people who share their problems with us. Whether it's your spouse, your children, or your friends, it's hard *not* to get involved in their problems. People have told me that, after listening to someone vent, they cannot help but bring some of their loved ones' negativity into their own days. Realize that the negative aspects of their lives don't have to become a part of yours. You will have someone you care about go through a tough time and need a willing ear so that they can safely vent their stresses. Listen, empathize, and give them positive feedback. Utilize warmth and understanding, but if you find that their situation is draining you, you will need to distance yourself from their words. While you may listen to them and sympathize with them, do not let them drain your positive energy. If the negativity is coming from a close relative (spouses, children, or parents), ease away softly. Make a positive comment and then physically leave, hang up the phone, or end the communication. Once you have established whether someone is only having a low moment or if that particular person is negative overall, you can either help that person to find the positive outlook they are lacking or minimize the amount of time you spend with them for your own sake. You will need to tap into your positive energy reserves so that you can release the burden of their negative energy without letting it affect you. In other cases, the best way to maintain your sanity and positive outlook, unfortunately, would be to release your loved one and pray that he or she finds the missing ingredients that are key to being happy.

There has to be an emotional incentive to maintain your relationships. There have been thousands of divorces and people leaving their jobs because they can't continue on surrounded by the negativity of the other person or company. Those who find relational and occupational success figure out how to live in the moment and work around negativity.

Every day, energy drainers are competing with your thoughts to be in the moment. You decide if you want to acknowledge these negative emotions and how much energy and attention you give them. The emotions that are the largest energy drainers are worry, fear, greed, hate, guilt, anger, and stress. Whether it's fear about an event coming up, anxiety over the reactions of people around you, anger that you "didn't get the part/job," or greed, these negative feelings sap away your energy quicker than anything else.

One of the biggest emotional energy drainers, in my opinion, is a lack of forgiveness. To hold a grudge against someone or a situation continually holds you back from living a full and happy life. It gives someone else incredible power over your life, since you can't forgive them and move on. Can you do anything to keep negative events from happening, such as an argument with a colleague, or a disagreement with your spouse? Probably not. Instead, you have to deal with each situation as it comes along. Constantly worrying about stressful situations that may or may not be in your power to control can be incredibly stressful.

One of my clients called me the other day and, as she started talking, I knew instantly that she wasn't happy. "What's the matter?" I asked her in concern. She replied that she'd lost her sense of taste for the last week or so. While this was a medical problem that I obviously couldn't solve for her, I couldn't leave her in a negative moment. "Isn't there anything that you can count as a blessing?" I brought up the fact that her other senses were still working. After giving her a moment or two of encouragement, I could hear the change in her voice that indicated she was smiling. She was laughing when I said good-bye a few moments later.

Make a commitment to become more positive. Practice some of these ideas, and reflect on some of my experiences. Decide if you will take the easy, negative path or the path that makes not only you feel better about your life, but will also help other people to feel good.

Just One
Author Unknown

One song can spark a moment,
One flower can wake the dream.
One tree can start a forest,
One bird can herald spring.
One smile begins a friendship,
One handclasp lifts a soul.
One star can guide a ship at sea,
One word can frame the goal.
One vote can change a nation,
One sunbeam lights a room.
One candle wipes out darkness,
One laugh will conquer gloom.
One step must start each journey,
One word must start each prayer.
One hope will raise our spirits,
One touch can show you care.
One voice can speak with wisdom,
One heart can know what's true.
One life can make a difference,
You see, it's up to you!

Step 4: Don't Give Up!

·····

Whenever you find yourself doubting how far you can go, just remember how far you have come. Remember everything you have faced, all the battles you have won, and all the fears you have overcome.

—UNKNOWN

WHEN I WAS in the Marine Corps boot camp, there were times that I thought I was going to quit. During the daily runs when my feet were blistered, my lungs were burning, and physical exhaustion overcame me, I would think of taking the easy way out and quitting. With my next thought, I would then envision myself standing tall at graduation, proving that I had achieved an impossible goal. This image kept me going through boot camp, and I left there a stronger person, both physically and mentally.

If there were a medicine I could recommend that would help you release negativity, I would. However, there's no pill that can cure a negative thinker. Since there is no simple fix, I think that's reason in itself to say good-bye to negativity. Honestly, you don't always have to feel like you are full of energy. It's normal to go through the day and wind up feeling empty simply because of everyday occurrences and encounters. Your energy supply, though, is never completely empty; there is such a thing as a second and third wind.

How many times have you or people you know encountered a bump in the road and turned it into an insurmountable mountain? We get worked up about minor events or situations, and we can ruin potential moments in the process. Spending every moment you have on those bumps in life will only distract you from the moment at hand, draining your energy level and leaving you unwilling to capture this moment's energy.

Expending your energy on positive actions during the day automatically refills your energy tank. As you expend your energy by doing tasks each moment at a time, your energy supply drains but is just as quickly stimulated by positive thoughts, actions, and words, both to yourself and to others. As long as you believe you have energy, you've got it!

Your body is always producing energy for you—

you've just got to learn to conserve it. No one wants to carry around a twenty-pound bag of groceries indefinitely, but that's what you do to yourself mentally by carrying around excess negative baggage. Someone else's problems, even though they're not yours, can dampen your positivity. Your guilt over what you could have, would have, or should have done may crush your positive thoughts. Your fears and worries about the uncontrollable future will hamper any movement toward leaving your comfort zone.

My oldest son trained for almost a year to complete a full ironman race. He would train for hours every day so that he was prepared for the grueling 140-mile course consisting of a two-and-a-half-mile swim, 112 miles of biking, and a full-marathon-distance run. He convinced himself that he was an iron man, and he was determined to finish the course before the cut-off time.

Not only did he finish the race, but he finished it in about fourteen hours, less time than he had predicted he would need. He didn't give up on himself, and he finished the challenging course with a feeling of irreplaceable pride. I'm proud to have been there to watch.

Once you adapt some of the philosophies I've outlined here to your own life, you will obtain more energy and positivity. I've advised married couples who have confided in me regarding some conflict to simply reach out and ask each other, "How can we get back to love?" After four decades of marriage, I can assure you that, by deciding that you can enjoy each moment of being in love with someone, you can feel great and energized by simply remaining with someone who you know loves you because you don't give up on each other. In relationships, one of my solutions to messy situations is to say, "I'm positive I will work things out." Then, I can work with those who have negative feelings and say to them, "I am positive we can work this out."

Believe you have an endless supply of energy, and you will. It doesn't happen by magic but by having the mind-set to live in the moments of life. Don't give up! We all have that endless supply of energy, and I hope that you are able to access yours so that you can achieve whatever you set your mind to.

The Optimist Creed

Promise Yourself:

To be so strong that nothing can disturb your
peace of mind.

To talk health, happiness, and prosperity to
every person you meet.

To make all your friends feel that there is
something in them that is wonderful.

To look at the sunny side of everything and
make your optimism come true.

To think only of the best, to work only for
the best, and to expect only the best, and
to be just as enthusiastic about the success
of others as you are about your own.

To forget the mistakes of the past and press
on to the greater achievements of the
future.

To wear a cheerful countenance at all times
and give every living creature you meet a
smile.

To give so much time to the improvement of
yourself that you have no time to criticize
others.

To be too large for worry, too noble for anger,
too strong for fear, and too happy to
permit the presence of trouble.

Step 5: When in Doubt, Smile

· · · · ·

Your most valuable resource to keep yourself energized is a sincere smile!
—PAUL THOMPSON

THE POWER OF a smile is perhaps the best-kept secret in the world. It is one of the most common symbols among people conveying a desire to connect, to reach out, and to form a tentative bond of communication. The power of a smile can make anyone who receives it relax and feel good, and in turn, it makes you feel good as well.

When you see a cheerful person, someone who greets you with a smile and a warm greeting, pay that person a compliment. Say something like, "You generate so much positive energy." Most times, that person will tell you that you have made his or her day.

I have found that instead of using up all of my energy ridding myself completely of negative energy, I can set a mental boundary around my positive thoughts and not let those negative thoughts through. It has been extremely helpful for me to write down the emotions I feel because of someone negative in my life. Once I have written down my feelings, I can reflect on how to move forward. By writing down what caused me to feel so much negativity, I also notice that I begin to feel more positive almost immediately.

There's a positive and negative side to everything and everybody! While motivational books like this one will help dispel your negative thoughts and feelings, it's up to you and your own inner strength to make sure that you remain positive once you've rid yourself of the negativity. Stop for a minute and look objectively at your emotions. By not giving negative thoughts power to be energy-drainers, you'll have more energy each day and enjoy the moments of your life so much more. For every negative thought that pops into your mind, look for a positive substitute for it.

It takes forty-three muscles to frown, but only seventeen to smile. When life throws a curve ball at you, how you field it determines whether or not you're going to be drained of your energy or energized by an infusion of it. "What if" scenarios can deplete us like a leak in our tires. "What if the train is late?" "What if the power goes out?" "What if I'm late for work again?" No matter what is going through your mind or what is happening around you, don't dwell on the negative. You have to learn from mistakes and problems, not think about them constantly. If you dwell on all of the bad things that could happen, you don't leave much room for positive thoughts, and your energy level will deplete.

Recently, I was at the airport preparing to fly to a seminar in California when we received news of a terrorist threat in England. While I did expect delays, I hadn't expected to miss two flights while waiting to go through security. Finally, they put me on a standby flight, but, in the meantime, the general atmosphere of the bustling airport was filled with worry, fear, and confusion. I tried to keep a smile on my face while I waited, speaking with people around me and turning some of their fearful, worried thoughts to calm, positive feelings. As we wound our way through the airport corridor, people that I had reached out to would smile and thank me. I knew that their positivity resulted from their interaction with me. Many of us who were waiting in that interminable line were able to turn a distressing setback into a situation that was bearable. Eventually, eight hours later, I was able to get on my flight. Those long hours of waiting were certainly unplanned, but the contacts I made and the positive feelings I shared enabled me to keep my own thoughts positive.

One of my favorite things to do is to smile at strangers. Their responses vary from a smile out of reflex to one out of surprise because not many people think to smile at people they don't know. A smile opens the door of communication with others; it can make a difference in your interaction with someone and in the overall demeanor of this communication. A smile is powerful enough to change negative feelings to positive.

If you get involved in volunteer organizations and charity work, you will have the opportunity to spread positive thoughts and smiles to those who need it the most. You will also feel incredible about your own self. Consciously feed your mind positive energy, and you'll be amazed at the results.

If you are dreading an upcoming event, such as an evaluation or a family gathering, picture a positive scenario that you want to happen instead of what you are worrying about, and you may be surprised at what you find. Perhaps your evaluation will be better than you'd hoped, or crazy Uncle Charlie might forget to show up, thus saving you and the rest of the family stress. Most things that we worry will happen, never happen!

Don't worry, and don't forget to smile.

Step 6: Release Your Anger

• • • • •

Anyone can become angry—that is easy, but to be angry with the right people to the right degree, at the right time, for the right purpose and for the right way—that is not easy.

—ARISTOTLE

ANGER IS AN emotion that flames out when someone "steps on our toes," either verbally or literally. Anger acts like a fire, and the more you fuel it, the hotter it gets. If you allow someone to make you angry, they are controlling you and the situation. Don't give control of your emotions to others! Only you have full control of your emotions, and when you remain calm, you make the situation better for all involved. Remember, when two people are arguing or fighting, both people have to take responsibility. Two wrongs never make a right!

I told my children as they were growing up that if two people were arguing, two people were wrong. While it may sound old-fashioned, I still have my children use the phrase, "Temper, temper!" if they see me begin to lose my temper. When I am angry, I count to ten so that I don't lose my temper toward the offending person or situation. There are times when I have to extend that ten to twenty or more, but not often.

If someone is angry and throws their anger towards you and you catch it rather than deflect it, ask yourself why you keep letting the person anger you. instead of working on the relationship. Counting and taking deep breaths help me to stay calm, whether my feelings are justified or not. Rationally, I know that if all individuals gave themselves license to lose their tempers over anything, this world would be a miserable place, indeed. After I calm down, I look back to see what actually triggered these feelings of anger. Was it someone else's anger that triggered my anger? Or did I simply use anger as the easiest way to handle the frustration of the moment? Anger loves to stay with us and consume our energy. Some people in this world hold their anger close to their hearts, and these are the people you want to keep at a safe distance. I have found that simply being in the same company as these incredibly angry people makes me feel on edge. Additionally, by conversing with them, I feel their anger and unwillingly find myself becoming angry. If it looks like a skunk, smells like a skunk, and acts like a skunk—it's a skunk. In the same vein, if the person looks angry, talks angrily, and won't let things go—you get my meaning. Just walk away if any effort you make to infuse calm into the situation fails.

There will be times when you may feel adrift amid a storm of anger, negative stress, pain, grief, or frustration, and it's very difficult stay positive in the moment. How you handle negativity at these times is key to maintaining your balance. Remember, first, that even though you may feel horrible inside, these negative emotions are only temporary. Eventually, you will regain your mental equilibrium. Only by constantly thinking about your negative thoughts will you find yourself feeling drained, weak, and dispirited.

If you're angry with someone, talk out your frustration with that person as soon as possible. If that is not feasible, draw that person on paper (as well as you're able to), and work out your frustrations with the piece of paper. You'll feel calmer after you list reasons for the dissension because you've released your negative energy in a safe and drama-free way.

There are always going to be triggers for anger, and I try to remind myself to stay calm and think about why those tripped triggers are allowing my temper to flare up. To defend against anger both in yourself and in others, take a step away from the negativity before it envelops you, remember that it takes a huge amount of energy to maintain anger, and find the courage to approach and either apologize or forgive. If you are unable to meet face-to-face with the person you have negative feelings toward, picture him or her in your mind and explain why you feel angry. Then let go of the anger, and dig deep for your smile. You will feel so much better!

Count your blessings,
Instead of your crosses;
Count your gains,
Instead of your losses;
Count your joys,
Instead of your woes;
Count your friends,
Instead of your foes.

—Unknown

Step 7: Diminish Greed, Jealousy, and Fear

·····

If you are depressed, you are living in the past.
If you are anxious, you are living in the future.
If you are at peace, you are living in the present.
—LAO TZU

GREED IS ONE of those addictive, continuous feelings that initially motivates and propels us, but, like candy, it gives us only short-term bursts of energy so that we're never satisfied. Greed draws endlessly on your energy supply. Wanting the newest car, wanting a bigger house, wanting more money—all are ways to increase happiness, but for how long? What happens when a newer model or style comes out? You'll need even more money to pay for them.

Is it really worth it? Do you want to equate having things with increasing happiness?

No matter what your station is in life, greed is always ready to depress and drain you because you don't have whatever you're wishing for at the moment.

Jealousy is similar to greed because it wants something someone else has, but jealousy has even further reaching tentacles.

There is no good use for jealousy in your life because it is such a huge waste of energy and time. Think about it: if you feel that someone else is in a better situation than you are, why not look at your own life and see what you could change to make it better?

If you find that you are debilitated by fear, you need to address it. We fear things like falling, failing, or unknowns. Sometimes talking about your fears with someone else will help you either to dissipate them or to stop dwelling on them so intensely so that you can move on and complete the tasks that are before you.

For example, during a flight, we hit a rough patch of turbulence, and I found myself thinking about my chances of survival. Although a statistical study of the probabilities of crashing (more highway deaths occur per year than those resulting from airplane crashes) would have helped to ease my fears, the information was not available to me and couldn't help me at that moment. Instead, it was up to me to handle my fear. First, I commanded my body to relax. Then, I talked to myself about how safe airplane flights actually are. I've been on hundreds of flights and never had more than a bout of turbulence affect me. I also reminded myself that worrying would not help me in the situation so it would be better to relax and dwell on positive thoughts. Next, I made small talk with the people around me (a good distraction!), and, eventually, we landed safely, much to my great relief. That fear will always be there for me, but I know how to deal with it.

There are many kinds of unhealthy fears or phobias, and you can take that first step toward conquering them by thinking positively. I often hear people afraid of flying talking about their upcoming flights with dread before they've even gone anywhere. You will not benefit from spending months thinking about a fear. That only drains your energy and may even give you an unrelenting anxiety attack. In perspective, fear reminds us there is uncertainty; it is telling us that we're at risk. By dwelling on our fears, we tend to magnify them to the point that some people won't ever face their fears because of their fright that something will happen to them.

Laird Gutterson, a retired colonel in the air force who lived through five years as a prisoner of war, shared a story with me about how he survived that situation, despite his fear. Gutterson knew that if he were to survive, he had to feel hope. Daily, he summoned the image of his young daughter throwing her arms around his neck and saying, "I love you, Daddy!" That vision would flood him with waves of intense unconditional love and kept him strong throughout his ordeal.

In order to face fear, you need courage. I was motivated by one of my friends, Vincent, who was recently diagnosed with a brain tumor. On the night I met him for dinner, he had approximately six weeks to live. I have to admit that I originally felt uneasy because I felt sorry for him and didn't know what would be appropriate to talk about with a dying man. I worried for nothing, though, since Vincent was the one who did most of the talking. He was so full of life that I wanted to capture some of his enthusiasm. I had assumed that he wouldn't want to talk about death or dying, but I was wrong there, too. He talked openly about it, and, in fact, he still believed that he had a chance of beating the cancer. All evening, he had a smile on his face that spoke of confidence and courage.

He was concerned about a young friend of his, though, a senior at the local high school who happened to be sickly, even though he looked healthy and strong. One day at the clinic where they were both getting treatment, Vincent approached him and tried to interest the young man in conversation, to find some tiny spark of shared interest so that they could talk. After a few tries, the young man turned to him and asked him how he could be so friendly and happy in a treatment facility.

"I'm doomed!" the young man told my friend.

Vincent pondered this for a moment and then asked him how he got to be in such fine shape. The young man told him that he was the cocaptain of the wrestling team and that he had won many matches against opposing high schools. Vincent asked him how he felt when he won, if he picked up his chin proudly and walked around with confidence. The young man replied that he did. Vincent told him that life gives all of us a bad deal at times, but we are in control of everything if we have the right frame of mind and the courage to face whatever comes our way. He told the young man that, if you want to be an "up" kind of person, you have to think that you are a winner *all* of the time, not just when you actually win something.

The next time that Vincent saw the young man at the treatment center, he seemed to be in a better frame of mind to deal with his illness, with a more positive mind-set. Note that many doctors will tell you that this is an important aspect in speeding up the recovery process.

Knowing that you can overcome your fears by

addressing them will stop this overwhelming, negative emotion from draining your energy source. Reducing the amount of greed, jealousy, and fear in your life will enable you to fully appreciate each day so much more.

If-
by Rudyard Kipling

If you can keep your head when all about you
Are losing theirs and blaming it on you;
If you can trust yourself when all men doubt
you,
But make allowance for their doubting too;
If you can wait and not be tired by waiting,
Or, being lied about, don't deal in lies,
Or, being hated, don't give way to hating,
And yet don't look too good, nor talk too
wise;
If you can dream—and not make dreams
your master;
If you can think—and not make thoughts
your aim;
If you can meet with triumph and disaster
And treat those two imposters just the same;
If you can bear to hear the truth you've
spoken
Twisted by knaves to make a trap for fools,
Or watch the things you gave your life to
broken,
And stoop and build 'em up with wornout
tools;
If you can make one heap of all your
winnings

And risk it on one turn of pitch-and-toss,
And lose, and start again at your beginnings
And never breath a word about your loss;
If you can force your heart and nerve and
sinew
To serve your turn long after they are gone,
And so hold on when there is nothing in you
Except the Will, which says to them: "Hold
on";
If you can talk with crowds and keep your
virtue,
Or walk with kings—nor lose the common
touch;
If neither foes nor loving friends can hurt
you;
If all men count with you, but none too
much;
If you can fill the unforgiving minute
With sixty seconds' worth of distance run—
Yours is the Earth and everything that's in it,
And—which is more—you'll be a Man my
son!

Step 8: Stop Being a Guilt Catcher

· · · · ·

The key is to keep company only with people who uplift you, whose presence calls forth your best.

—EPICTETUS

BELIEVE EVERYONE CARRIES around some measure of guilt, whether it's for something they did or didn't do, laid-on guilt by a family member or friend, or guilt because they haven't measured up to some societal standard. How we handle our feelings of guilt and whether we let it fester inside us determines how much it will ultimately drain our energy. If we can let go of this negative emotion, it will not affect us.

We all know people who act listless and depressed, especially those people who carry around their guilt like a banner that reads, "I'm to blame." Some people hold onto others' blame and carry it with them continuously.

If you are carrying guilt around each day, my advice is to tackle the issue—whether or not it's guilt you ought to own—and dissolve the guilt by forgiving yourself. If there's a way to increase your love for yourself and the people who were affected by your actions, do it and move forward.

Again, as with all energy drainers, turn your mind in a more positive direction and think about something different. Avoid having your guilt be something you carry with you in your mind. It will only become heavier and heavier.

Let's say, for example, that you are looking forward to an event taking place that night. You are happy because it will be a positive experience with people you enjoy.

Once you arrive, you notice Tom Thundercloud coming toward you in the hallway. He always has something negative to say. He approaches you and begins to rant and rave about this and that, what someone said to him and how horrible he is feeling. You listen to him, feeling somewhat guilty because you want to walk away but you can't, and, what's worse, you begin to feel his negative energy drain you.

Stop! Bring yourself into the moment and focus on what's in your world and only your world. Let Tom Thundercloud go rain on someone else while you think of how you can get back to being positive. Envision the sticky residue of negativity he has left behind being washed away from your mind.

There are people in this world who are "guilt throwers" and others who are very adept at being "guilt catchers." Please know that no one is perfect, and a simple mistake (such as forgetting to call the florist or pick up clothes from the cleaners) is not significant enough to have a guilt trip over. Don't be a guilt catcher—brush guilt feelings away and know that you are doing the best you can. Someone will try to make you feel guilty for not doing something for them, but no one has the power to make you feel guilty except yourself—and dry cleaning is not worth it! Once you forgive yourself, you'll find that you don't dwell on the incident as much, and you won't let it drain your energy source either. Feeling good about forgiving yourself will dispel any feelings of inadequacy you may be feeling.

Life decisions are yours to make; no one should make you feel guilty for making a decision that is not what they feel is the right decision. If you really don't want to do something or go somewhere, that is your decision to make. Realize that many people will try to give you a guilt trip because they're not happy with the way you are living your life. Maybe you are doing something your way and not the way they perceive to be the right way, and they will guilt you into thinking their way is the best way. This is where you take your stand and let their ideas go through one ear and out the other so you can live your moment the way you want to. Everything that has happened in our lives influences how we move forward. Say goodbye to guilt and regret. Practice destroying negative images and don't spend too much time worrying about them. If you don't give them a chance to take over your life, they will eventually fade.

Carrying guilt is sometimes referred to as "taking a guilt trip." While this is only a cliché, think about it for a moment: Is a guilt trip something you really want to take in your life? Go on a trip to the Bahamas—Europe—anywhere but a guilt trip!

Life Is
by Mother Theresa

Life is an opportunity, benefit from it.
Life is beauty, admire it.
Life is a dream, realize it.
Life is a challenge, meet it.
Life is a duty, complete it.
Life is a game, play it.
Life is a promise, fulfill it.
Life is sorrow, overcome it.
Life is a song, sing it.
Life is a struggle, accept it.
Life is a tragedy, confront it.
Life is an adventure, dare it.
Life is luck, make it.
Life is too precious, do not destroy it.
Life is life, fight for it.

Step 9: Increase Your Energy Reserves

·····

I will personally guarantee that adding any form of exercise to your day will double your energy reserves and reduce your stress dramatically, as well as tripling your personal feelings of self-esteem and happiness.

—PAUL THOMPSON

USING YOUR ENERGY on positive actions during the day automatically refills your energy tank! When you start your day, whenever you arise, your mind and body are rested. I suggest to people to stand in front of the mirror the minute they rise from their beds so that they can give themselves the affirmations that they are great and will have a good day. Most happy, energetic, and motivated people do this, and we boost our day right from the start.

I could write endlessly on the benefits of regular exercise and a nutritional diet. I've found that people who already exercise on a regular basis don't have to be convinced on how much more energy they have because of exercise. Those who follow a healthy diet know the benefits of eating good foods for their body and their overall health as well. There's no sense for me to quote facts and figures about the doctors or medical reports to you because you already know how good exercise is for your body and your mind. I can confirm that you will have more energy if you start exercising. For beginners, try taking small daily walks at first, and slowly build up your routine until it is a habit that you look forward to each day to make you feel great.

You may hear of someone who has had a heart attack, and then, within the next few months, he is out there in your neighborhood running four to six miles daily. How is this possible? That person is not suddenly doing exercise for energy (which is definitely a by-product) but because he believes that exercise might let him enjoy a few more years of life. Exercise is also an antidote to depression and helps you to weather emotionally low periods until the sun shines again.

Whether you are exercising by yourself or with a friend, or even a group of people who meet for an exercise class several times a week, you are helping yourself to feel better and live longer. So-called miracle energy pills or weight loss aids will never have the same effect as taking a walk or hiking with your dog.

My eldest son was an athlete in high school, but it wasn't until his thirties that he discovered running. He has been running for several years, not only to maintain a healthy weight but also because he feels so much better about himself after a run.

He has completed the New York City Marathon four times and is on track to complete a race in each of the fifty states with his wife. My younger son is an avid hiker, and he's always looking for the next mountain or path to explore. He finds the hikes strenuous but necessary to clear his mind and to refresh himself to deal with the everyday stressors in life.

My youngest daughter went through a tough divorce, and, when the dust settled, she found the stress level in her life was very high, especially with three young children, a house, and all of the responsibilities that were now hers alone to deal with. She began to jog, slowly at first, then more often. At the urging of my oldest, she signed up for her first half-marathon almost a year after the divorce was finalized and finished it with a huge smile on her face. Running was her escape from the emotional and mental scars the divorce had left her with, and today she is a completely different person. She talks to as many people as she can about how running has changed her life, and her enthusiasm is contagious!

My older daughter sees every new day as a gift. She is constantly researching ways to keep her body healthy after being diagnosed with Type I Diabetes at nineteen months and became a nurse in order to help people.

I recently began a yoga class and highly recommend it as a way to relax and to learn how to feel the energy around you. Check it out, even if it sounds like an exercise that isn't right for you. For those who do yoga consistently, it's a fulfilling and energizing boost for the body and the mind.

Get outside, smell the fresh air, feel the wind against your face. Walk—or jog—in the moment, and you will be rewarded. Exercise gives you more energy and a more positive feeling about your body. Make sure you have your music with you as well. Music is a definite mood booster, and new technology allows you to make your own playlists depending on what kind of mood you are in. Historically, it was the blaring music that gave soldiers energy and adrenaline to push forward on the battlefield. From bagpipes and drums, to horns and flutes, music would infuse a battle cry with energy to keep the soldiers moving forward.

I cannot forget standing on that beach in North Carolina, waiting with my son and all the other contenders for the Ironman to start. The Eminem song "Lose Yourself" blared through the speakers, sending shivers through the crowd and motivating the men and women to be confident that they would, indeed, finish the race.

My father was eighty-three when he died, and, while he did feel the typical eighty-three-year-old aches and pains, when one of his favorite songs came on the radio, he became as energized as the Energizer bunny! I, myself, have had to be dragged away from the dance floor after a few hours or more. I just love to dance!

I recommend that you put your favorite songs on a MP3 player or an iPod and listen to them whenever possible. As I'm typing these words, I have my "feel good" songs playing on my computer, and my toe is happily tapping along to the beat.

Your definition of "good" music may be different from mine, but by choosing music that helps you gain energy, you are increasing your level of feeling alive, whether you are exercising at the time or not!

Don't Quit
Anonymous

When things go wrong, as they sometimes
will,
When the road you're trudging seems all
uphill,
When the funds are low and the debts are
high,
And you want to smile but you have to sigh,
When care is pressing you down a bit,
Rest if you must, but don't you quit.
Life is queer with its twists and its turns,
As every one of us sometimes learns,
And many a failure turns about
When they might have won, had they stuck
it out.
Don't give up though the pace seems slow,
You may succeed with another blow.
Often the goal is nearer than
It seems to a fain and faltering man.
Often the struggler has given up
When he might have captured the victor's
cup
And he learned too late when the night came
down,
How close he was to the golden crown.
Success is failure turned inside out

The silver tint of the clouds of doubt.
And you never can tell how close you are,
It may be near when it seems so far;
So stick to the fight when you're hardest hit,
It's when things seem worse that you must
not quit!

Step 10: Create Passion with Positive Thinking

· · · · ·

Having passion in your life's moments will give you an endless supply of energy.

—PAUL THOMPSON

SOME PEOPLE CALL my philosophy about living in the moment one of the best motivational tools they've encountered. "What a great motivator you are, Paul!" is something that I enjoy hearing often. I've trained many corporate people in my career, and when I meet up with them down the road, they always tell me that it was my energy and motivation that gave them confidence to achieve their goals.

Positive thinking depends on how the individual chooses to see things in life. When you feel that all you can find and focus on are negative thoughts, it's probably time to make some changes in both your actions and your thought patterns. One key asset toward change (one that I've been noted to have) is abundance of passion for life. When you become passionate, you're more energized for everything in your life. You can't force passion to just happen, though. Passion comes from loving what you do, having faith in yourself and a higher being, and believing in the innate talents and individual qualities we all possess.

There are times when I feel that I have to turn my positive energy down a notch, especially with new people I meet. From feedback I've received from various clients and friends, I've discovered that my outgoing personality can be interpreted as overzealous, superficial, or too much for others to handle at times. Therefore, when I'm meeting with a new client, I will sometimes hold back on projecting my full energy level until I get to know them better. Sometimes, people are wary when they first meet me because of my happy, carefree attitude. It seems that they are so accustomed to negativity that they are not ready to experience someone with my innate contentment with life.

Eventually, my smile is able to work its magic on even the most stubborn person. I get my energy from being able to boost other people's energy levels, whether it's with a smile, a kind word, or a hug or a touch on the arm, to show them that I am connected to them.

Those that come back for a second meeting tell me how they are impressed by my positive energy and caring attitude. This is the number-one reason I believe I've been so successful in my chosen career—people trust me for their financial security and sense that I truly listen and honestly care. Many people tell me their personal problems as well as their financial problems, making sometimes feel like a priest!

Jeff Keller, a friend of mine who is also an author and motivational speaker, wrote a great book about attitude being everything. One of his main themes is not to think or dwell on the negative. I have followed his advice and seen results in myself as well as in others who I know are familiar with his material.

Some people never use the passion that we are all born with simply because they are unaware that it is inside them. Although I can't tell you what your passion is, your subconscious mind knows and is willing to share it with you if you would just open the door to it.

When you focus on having a passionate life, you will automatically start recognizing what will make you happy and more energized. Perhaps you feel strongly about a worthy cause, such as fighting cancer. Maybe, with everything inside you, you believe in an idea, and you do everything possible to make it happen. You may be a person for whom your occupation is also your passion. If you're really passionate about your dreams, aspirations, or lifestyle, seek out people who you feel can help you to reach your goals. In finding people with similar passions, you will find virtually a paved path for you to success and overall contentment.

I was attending a seminar at a local university when I noticed a man I knew sitting on a bench outside, looking absolutely exhausted. After I greeted him, I asked him what was going on. He proceeded to tell me that he had three more classes to teach before he could go home, and then he had to do some errands that night with his family.

"I don't know how I'm ever going to do this!" he said, his voice sounding defeated.

I paused for a moment then asked him where he would rather be.

"Oh, I don't know," he replied.

I persisted. "But if you really could be somewhere else, where would it be?"

This time, he paused before answering, considering his response. "I would really like to be in my own business, doing what I really like to do," he finally admitted.

I had him visualize his own business and what it could mean to him. I had him thinking of how great it would feel to be finally doing something he really wanted to do. As this positive thought exercise went on for another few minutes, he straightened on the bench. His posture changed from indicating a sad, dejected individual to an enthusiastic-looking man who had a goal he could both feel and excitedly think about. Ten minutes later, he shook my hand and walked away with a bounce in his step and an enthusiastic smile on his face.

By living in a positive moment, rather than dwelling on the many stressors in his life, he was able to access his energy supply. It wasn't really empty after all but still there, waiting for the right thoughts and positive thinking to release it. Add to this an increase in passion for what his future could be, and my friend was well on his way to achieving his long-time goal.

Keep your passion with you, and you will find that you will accept and nurture more positive thoughts and become stronger mentally and emotionally. Move forward with your passion, and you will find so many doors that will open and so many lives you can change, starting with your own.

If there's ever been a moment to follow your passion—it's now!

Part IV

Summary

Final Thoughts

· · · · ·

Believe in yourself! Have faith in your abilities!
Without a humble but reasonable confidence
in your own powers, you cannot be successful or
happy.

—NORMAN VINCENT PEALE

WHENEVER I TOLD people about this book I was writing, they would immediately show a spark of interest, particularly when I mentioned the theme of tapping into their positive thoughts and energy levels. I believe that most people are looking for ways to have more energy and to be happier in their lives.

In the same way that you can visualize all the things that can go wrong, you can just as easily visualize success. While you encounter numerous obstacles each day, you are in control of your thoughts. It's your choice to read this book, your choice to follow a few of my suggestions, and your choice to live in the moments.

Overall, I feel that you can improve your life, your relationships, and your circumstances simply by changing key thought processes. No matter what happens, you should always remember that a healthy attitude can work wonders on any given situation.

The key is to keep your thoughts positive; stay away from negative people; and focus on the future rather than the past. Find what makes you happy, and keep that happiness in your life. Don't worry about what other people think or do. The main key to finding more energy and living in the moment successfully is to do what makes you feel more energized and positive.

I also believe that I'm helping others by simply being a positive person. I think that, by offering my own energy to others through my words, facial expressions, and body language, I increase their energy levels. I cannot give you an exact number of people that I have helped, but I feel that I have succeeded in boosting hundreds (maybe even thousands!) of other people's energy levels for at least the amount of time that I was with them.

In his book *Meditations for Men Who Do Too Much*, Dean Acheson writes, "Perhaps the best thing about the future is that it only comes one day at a time." He continues:

We must learn to anticipate positive thoughts in a different, gentler light. The future is in five minutes, as well as next April or next year. Today is yesterday's future, and we must set out inner "expectation clocks" back from time to time. Frantically planning ahead only works if your day is devoid of happiness and serenity. Today, truly, is the future.

The future should be considered as a potential positive moment. Having a future goal in mind is great, especially if you can see yourself achieving that goal. Congratulate yourself on achieving your goals as well.

We do have to prepare ourselves for what tomorrow brings, but you can't prepare for tomorrow by worrying about it. Believe that you can handle anything that comes along. This enables you to continue living in the present, living in the moment, which is a success for you. You need to have the techniques to handle negativity, and the willingness to face any problems that arise head-on before they become a source of pessimism in your life.

Finally, you need to know that this book isn't the magic pill to give you everlasting energy. My goal is to have you think about what's really important in your life. Once you figure out where to focus your energy, you've made the first step of what will be many in the right direction.

I keep a book of positive quotes on my desk at home and one at my office. In my car, I have small books of positive affirmations. I keep cassettes and CDs readily available as my help line, and I know positive people who will energize me if I simply reach out to them with a phone call. If you can teach yourself how to view life in a more positive manner, then you will truly be on the path to enjoying happiness and energy in your life.

Tomorrow isn't promised to anyone, but when you follow these techniques, I promise you that your future days and moments will be as happy and energizing as you want them to be!

PT

by Sharon Gurecki

H OW MANY PEOPLE do you influence in a day? Just one day, one instant, where what you say or do can make the difference between someone feeling despair and someone feeling joy?

How many lives do you feel that you have changed for the better, just by being you?

By being happy, outgoing, wise, and caring.

Think of what this world would be like if you were never born.

If there was never a Paul Robert Thompson, kingly and handsome husband; adored and admired father; respected CFP; beloved son; grandfather of ten; and brother to six.

In that little house in South Jersey where in winter,

you froze; in summer, you baked; and in spring, you nearly drowned from the leaks in the ceiling.

What would that house have been like if you hadn't been there?

No older brother to tease his siblings, to track mud through the house, to sleep next to your father each and every night.

No one who played cowboys and Indians, who ran through the neighborhood with your sisters, cat-calling and making trouble, pushing over cows, and running through horse pastures in the dead of night.

No role model for your sisters, your brother;

No brave protector to banish rats from the corners, to rock to sleep a baby while your mother slept herself.

Imagine the difference there would have been, the emptiness in hearts that aren't quite sure what they're missing.

Fast-forward several years, years that weren't filled with your sunny smile, impish blue eyes, and dare-devil spirit.

Imagine Vietnam, 1965; you are not there to lead men who are frightened, scared, and unsure.

No one to make that first charge, to scout out a distant path, to share rations with fellow soldiers who may not have anything to eat or drink.

No one to lift the spirits of your comrades by initiating songs by campfires, by marching as straight and as proud as would befit a US Marine.

And the men, how many of them would have met an unpleasant death were it not for your bravery, your courage, your indomitable will and spirit?

If you weren't there, would the men who died so needlessly have felt that emptiness where you would have been?

Would they wonder what was missing?

When you were in the hospital recovering from a wound, didn't you boost the morale of your wounded comrades as they lay in their own miseries?

Didn't you share cookies with them?

If you hadn't been there, it would have been just another dreary day, of darkness in the midst of wartime.

And to think, if those cookies, which were sent to a cousin from a cousin in New Jersey, had reached the hands of someone else, some other lucky GI, then what would this world possibly be like?

Fate, as I see it, had you take those cookies and pass them around the ward, after which you requested the cousin's address.

If you hadn't written a letter to that cousin, the first of many, if you hadn't fallen in love through your correspondence, then what hell might this world be?

I certainly wouldn't know.

You made a pretty, loyal woman's life by being there for her to love.

If you hadn't decided to stay in New Jersey instead of riding off into the sunset, chasing your dream to California, if you hadn't been here to make that decision, who can tell what might be?

There would be one fewer father of three, your devoted son who is following in your footsteps;

One fewer loving daughter who chose to be a nurse and who now works with you, and whose son is a carbon copy of you.

There would be one fewer mother of three, a teacher, who has so much admiration and pride for the miles you've traveled, the obstacles you have overcome, and the goals you have achieved.

One fewer history lover, father of three, a son who respects and admires you in his own way.

But think, if you hadn't been there to love and marry a woman who would give you the world, to create four beautiful children who try in their own ways to show their immeasurable love for you, to influence countless people with your boundless energy, optimism, and love.

Think of all those kids whom you taught catechism to; the new financial planners whom you have mentored; and others who know that you can teach them so much about life.

How many people have you instilled strength

in, courage, the ability to handle complications; you instill morals and pride, and a wide-eyed look at the world along with an appreciation of the idea that the moment is now?

Think of the daily interactions you have, where people walk away with a smile and a "Thanks, Paul."

How many people do you influence in a day? How many lives have you changed for the better?

The truth is only too obvious to my eyes, yet another gift of your life.

Don't despair, for in times of trouble and hardship, you are a Thompson, a mighty, mighty Thompson, and it's a wonderful life.

About the Author

· · · · ·

Paul Thompson has been motivating and inspiring people for many years, both personally and professionally. He has helped hundreds of clients, family members, and friends discover their inner energy supplies, reach their goals, and live a positive life.

A former sergeant in the US Marine Corps and a Vietnam veteran, Paul works with organizations in providing assistance and guidance to wounded and disabled veterans. He has served as the senior vice president of CJM Planning Corporation and is the CEO/president of his own consulting company, Thompson & Thompson Consulting, Inc. He is also a professional motivational speaker, and has trained numerous people to be financial consultants who care.

Paul is a father of four and grandfather of ten. He is the author of *For My Grandchild*, a book of poetry inspired by his grandchildren. Paul currently lives in Franklin Lakes, New Jersey, with his wife of forty-six years, Karen, and is working on book number three.

CPSIA information can be obtained
at www.ICGtesting.com
Printed in the USA
FFOW05n1525040914

9 781627 871396